Finding Patterns

by Marilyn Deen

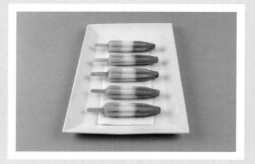

Consultant:
Adria F. Klein, PhD
California State University, San Bernardino

CAPSTONE PRESS
a capstone imprint

Wonder Readers are published by Capstone Press,
1710 Roe Crest Drive, North Mankato, Minnesota 56003.
www.capstonepub.com

Books published by Capstone Press are manufactured with paper
containing at least 10 percent post-consumer waste.

Library of Congress Cataloging-in-Publication Data
Deen, Marilyn.
   Finding patterns / Marilyn Deen. — 1st ed.
      p. cm. — (Wonder readers)
   Includes index.
   Summary: "Describes and explains the concept of patterns, including stripes, spots, and other repeating
designs"—Provided by publisher.
   ISBN 978-1-4296-7919-0 (paperback)
   ISBN 978-1-4296-8632-7 (library binding)
   1. Geometry in nature—Juvenile literature. 2. Pattern perception—Juvenile literature. I. Title.
   QA445.5.D436 2012
   152.14'23—dc23   2011022020

Note to Parents and Teachers

The Wonder Readers: Mathematics series supports national mathematics standards.
These titles use text structures that support early readers, specifically with a close
photo/text match and glossary. Each book is perfectly leveled to support the reader
at the right reading level, and the topics are of high interest. Early readers will
gain success when they are presented with a book that is of interest to them and is
written at the appropriate level.

Printed in the United States of America in North Mankato, Minnesota.
102011   006405CGS12

Table of Contents

Looking at Patterns........................4

Patterns in Spirals.........................8

Patterns from Dots 10

Patterns from Shapes....................12

Patterns from Lines......................14

Patterns and You..........................16

Glossary.......................................18

Now Try This! 19

Internet Sites 19

Index 20

Looking at Patterns

This fish has beautiful blue and yellow stripes. The stripes form a **pattern**. They are lines that repeat in the same way over and over again.

A pattern can be made of repeating shapes. Patterns can also be made of repeating colors. Some patterns have both repeating shapes and colors, like the stripes on this girl's shirt.

The shapes, colors, and numbers of things on this building form a pattern. Builders and artists often use patterns in the things they make. Scientists look for and study patterns in nature.

There are many patterns in this picture. Some have to do with shape, some with color, and some with number. See how many patterns you can find.

Patterns in Spirals

A **spiral** is a pattern that winds around in circles. The spiral in this shell is a repeating shape that gets bigger and bigger. The animal that lives in this shell makes the spiral as it grows and needs bigger "rooms" to live in.

This is a spiral staircase. You walk around and around to get from the bottom to the top. Look at the way the shell and the staircase are the same. Now look to see how they are different.

Patterns from Dots

Dots and spots are often part of a pattern. This bug has a pattern of black spots on its back.

These are **dominoes**. They are used for playing different games. In one game, players try to match the numbers and patterns of dots on the pieces.

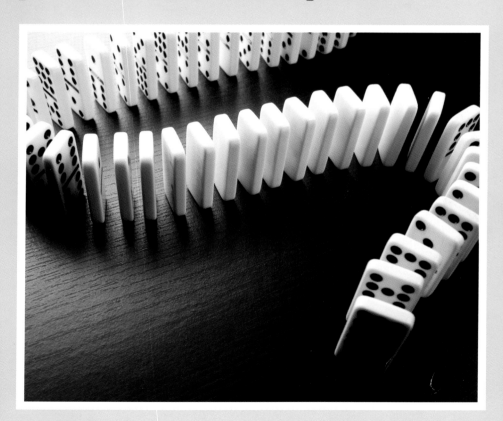

Patterns from Shapes

Bees keep the honey they make in a
honeycomb. A honeycomb is made of
beeswax. Each little room is filled with
honey. The rooms make a pattern.
Count the sides of each room to find
the pattern.

This **patchwork quilt** is a pattern made out of squares. Small squares are sewn together to make one big blanket. How many squares can you count?

Patterns from Lines

A spider made a pattern in this web. The pattern is made from threads of silk. Scientists study why and how spiders make patterns in their webs.

An artist is using colorful threads to make a rug. She is **weaving** a pattern with each thread. Describe the pattern you see.

Patterns and You

Everywhere you look, you can find new patterns. People and animals make patterns. Plants, artwork, buildings, and clothing all have designs in them.

If you pay attention, you can find patterns every day, no matter where you live or what you do. You might even create some patterns of your own. Keep looking at lines, colors, shapes, and numbers, and you will be surprised at the patterns that are all around you!

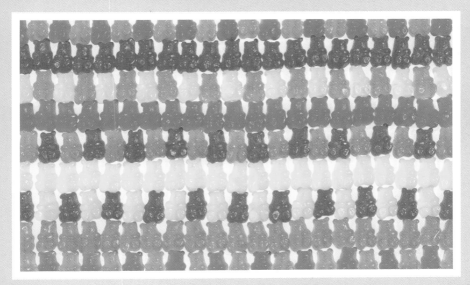

Glossary

dominoes   small rectangular tiles divided into two halves that are blank or contain dots

honeycomb   a wax structure made by bees and used by them to store honey; made of rows of six-sided "rooms"

patchwork quilt   a blanket made by stitching pieces of cloth together

pattern   colors, lines, shapes, or numbers that repeat in an orderly way

spiral   a pattern that winds around in circles

weaving   putting threads together to form a web, cloth, or rug

Now Try This!

Look for patterns on your clothing or in the classroom. Then go page by page through this book, looking for patterns around you that are similar to those in the book. Do you see any stripes, dots, squares, or spirals?

Internet Sites

FactHound offers a safe, fun way to find Internet sites related to this book. All of the sites on FactHound have been researched by our staff.

Here's all you do:

Visit *www.facthound.com*

Type in this code: 9781429686327

Index

animals, 4, 8, 10, 12, 14, 16

artists, 6, 15

builders, 6

circles, 8

clothing, 5, 16

colors, 5, 6, 7, 17

dots, 10, 11

games, 11

lines, 4, 17

nature, 6

numbers, 6, 7, 11, 17

scientists, 6, 14

shapes, 5, 6, 7, 17

spirals, 8-9

spots, 10

squares, 13

stripes, 4, 5

Editorial Credits

Maryellen Gregoire, project director; Mary Lindeen, consulting editor; Gene Bentdahl, designer; Sarah Schuette, editor; Wanda Winch, media researcher; Eric Manske, production specialist

Photo Credits

Capstone Studio: Karon Dubke, 1, 5, 16, 17; Shutterstock: Anatoly Tiplyashin, cover, Dejan Gileski, 6, Dmitry Oshchepkov, 4, Evoken, 13, Irina Tischenko, 10, 12, Michael Shake, 14, Mikhail Olykainen, 15, Natalia Macheda, 7, Sebastian Duda, 11, Stéphane Bidouze, 9, vvoronov, 8

Word Count: **429**   Guided Reading Level: **L**   Early Intervention Level: **17**